00594931

Bernadette
& the Lady
of Lourdes

ELEANOR GORMALLY

VERITAS

For Jim and Miriam, Jenny, James
and little Sarah

Published 2013 by
Veritas Publications
7–8 Lower Abbey Street
Dublin 1, Ireland
publications@veritas.ie
www.veritas.ie

ISBN 978-1-84730-513-8
Copyright © Eleanor Gormally, 2013
10 9 8 7 6 5 4 3 2 1
A catalogue record for this book is available
from the British Library.

Illustration and design by Barbara Croatto, Veritas
Printed in the Republic of Ireland by Hudson Killeen Limited

Veritas books are printed on paper made from the wood pulp of managed forests. For every tree felled, at least one tree is planted, thereby renewing natural resources.

Ecoutez! Now listen to the story I tell,
    it's a story worth hearing, so *ecoutez
    bien!*

One day in a village snuggled into a hill,
Three young girls leave home with baskets to fill.

With kindling and sticks, twigs of all
  kinds,
Counting fingers, they guess how much
  wood they will find.

They stop at the river, 'Yikes! The water
  is cold!'
Two wade in quickly, the third's not so
  bold.

Using stones as a bridge, both reach the
   far side,
'Bernadette Soubirous, come on over,'
   they chide.

She pulls off her socks; her feet make a
  splatter.
'If I catch a bad cold from it, what does
  it matter?'

Then something strange happens
  before Bernadette's eyes,
A mysterious vision takes her by
  surprise.

'*Mon Dieu,*' whispers Bernadette,
as the miracle unfolds.
And this is the story she
repeatedly told …

I heard the wind blowing,
The trees did not move.
Then a bright light surrounded
A hidden rock groove.

A beautiful Lady,
About my own size,
Stood right at the edge,
And looked straight in my eyes.

Her long dress was white,
Her sash azure blue.
On each foot a rose
Of deep golden hue.

Her greeting was soft,
She beckoned, 'Come near,'
Then stretched out her arms
And told me, 'Don't fear.'

I took out my Rosary,
Knelt down in that place.
Then prayed with the Lady
In silence and grace.

Aquero*, I called her,
My Lady in white.
I returned, as she asked me,
Throughout 'holy fortnight†'.

---

* *Aquero* is the word Bernadette used for the beautiful Lady she
   saw. It is a word in her own dialect.

† The Lady asked Bernadette to come to the grotto every day
   for two weeks. This became known as the 'holy fortnight'.

Her request was quite simple:
A chapel, a stream,
A place where all people
Could share in God's dream.

A place where there's healing
Of heart and of mind.
A place where there's peace
For each pilgrim
  to find.

Bernadette's story soon spread like
  wildfire,
Though some people doubted and
  called her a liar.

But crowds began following the
  teenager's steps,
Some watched and some gossiped,
  some wondered, some wept.

People brought candles that shimmered
  and danced,
Their faces lit up as they gazed on,
  entranced.

They too wished to witness the vision
  so holy,
But the Lady appeared to Bernadette
  solely.

Crowds came in their hundreds, they
  came night and day.
Yet some folk in the village warned
  people away.

'Don't go to the grotto,' they said
  cautiously,
'It's a practical joke, a trick! Can't you
  see?'

The town leaders' harsh questions made
   Bernadette nervous,
'We're wise, *ma petite*. You think you
   can fool us?'

But brave Bernadette found a calm
   deep inside.
She told them straight out, 'I have
   never once lied.'

'Her name is "Immaculate", my Lady in
  white.'
With these words the town leaders
  believed and grew quiet.

They knew that this young girl, both
  humble and poor,
Was telling the truth; they doubted no
  more.

So in that French village snuggled into
   a hill,
They built her the shrine – her wish
   they fulfilled.

To Lourdes pilgrims gathered – they
   gather there yet,
To honour Our Lady and the girl,
   Bernadette.

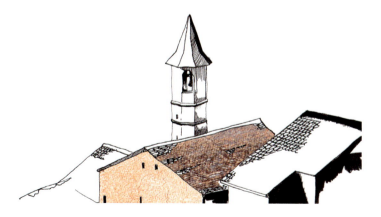

WHO WAS BERNADETTE?

- Bernadette Soubirous was born in Lourdes, France, on 7 January 1844.

- She was the daughter of a miller, François Soubirous, and a laundress, Louise Soubirous, and the eldest of four children.

- When Bernadette was a young teenager, her family became very poor and had to move to a one-roomed basement known as Le Cachot — 'the dungeon'.

- Bernadette first saw the Lady on 11 February 1858. She saw eighteen visions in total.

- In 1866, Bernadette joined the Sisters of Charity of Nevers in central France, becoming Sister Marie-Bernard. She worked there as an assistant in the hospital.

- Bernadette died on 16 April 1879.

- Pope Pius XI made Bernadette a saint on 8 December 1933.

Ireland

UK

Netherlands

Belgium

Germany

Paris

France

Switzerland

Italy

Lourdes

Spain

DID YOU KNOW?

- Lourdes is located in southern France, at the foot of the Pyrenees Mountains.
- Between four and six million people from all over the world visit Lourdes every year.
- More than two hundred million pilgrims have visited since 1860.
- Many people have been cured of their illnesses in Lourdes, with almost seventy of these being recognised as miracles by the Catholic Church.

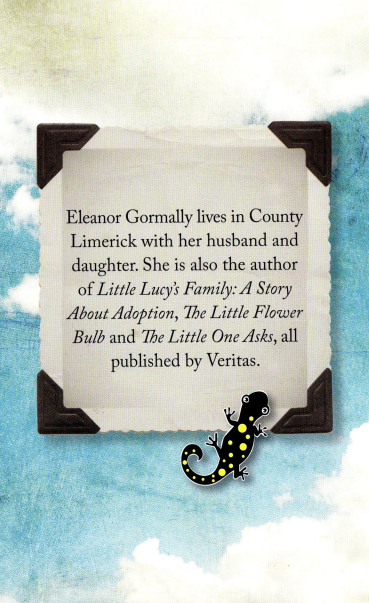

Eleanor Gormally lives in County Limerick with her husband and daughter. She is also the author of *Little Lucy's Family: A Story About Adoption*, *The Little Flower Bulb* and *The Little One Asks*, all published by Veritas.